A Leader's Guide to Ensuring Civility in a Hostile Political Environment

—————— Thomas Herzfeld ——————

DORRANCE
PUBLISHING CO
EST. 1920
PITTSBURGH, PENNSYLVANIA 15238

Dorrance Publishing Co
585 Alpha Drive
Pittsburgh, PA 15238
Visit our website at www.dorrancebookstore.com

ISBN: 978-1-6470-2383-6
eISBN: 978-1-6470-2788-9

A Leader's Guide
to Ensuring Civility in a
Hostile Political Environment

The majority of this work was published under the title, *How to Have a Civil Conversation in an Increasingly Uncivil and Hostile Environment*, copyright Thomas A. Herzfeld, 2018.

Table of Contents

Preface

For any leader to be successful, he or she must keep people in a cooperative spirit at all times. This is true for all types of leaders: business, governmental, military, religious, academic, and especially, heads of households. In the past several years, the political climate has become quite hostile. This polluted political environment has led to not only breakdowns in communication, but also a sense of national angst and division. We have fallen into a national "verbal gridlock" that prevents any useful or productive discussion of important issues and concepts.

Important and pressing problems are not being solved because we waste too much emotional and physical energy in name-calling and "trash talking." This has paralyzed government for some time already. Furthermore, political squabbling and infighting among employees could actually cripple a small business. Similarly, schools, churches, and even families are rendered dysfunctional by political antagonisms.

This has reached the point of a national emergency!

Good news! This book explains some of the root causes of the problem, but even better, it offers a viable solution. With care, courtesy, and civility, important topics can be discussed, and peace and relative tranquility can result. If your people can be civil, you can accomplish much more, whether in government, business, religion, school, or at home.

The 2020 election is fast approaching, and the media will be trying to get everyone riled up. So, fight back with a healthy dose of peaceful civility!

Take your time reading this short and concise treatment of a serious national problem. Read it twice, if necessary.

Thomas Herzfeld, MA
Woodland Park, NJ
September, 2019

Introduction

What Is the Problem Here?

It appears to me that the problem is largely about language. My high school Latin and Journalism teacher, James Powell, gave me great insight. He often stated, "A word is an idea." Every word is related to an idea in the user's mind. I believe that over the past 30 or 40 years, our linguistic skills have declined considerably. We are left with a large number of what I call "buzzwords," which people tend to throw around carelessly. (See the Appendix for a partial list.)

Each of these words has multiple meanings or even no meaning at all. They all, however, evoke strong (and immediate) emotional responses. Furthermore, they tend to mean different things to different people. Their meanings may have even changed drastically over time. Take the word "liberal" for example. Its meaning was much different in 1890 than in 1968. And today it has a different meaning than in the days of Hubert Humphrey and Nelson Rockefeller.

The biggest problem with the use of any of these buzzwords is the emotional response they cause. It almost always shuts down the thinking process and more often than not is a conversation ender. (The two parties often part with dislike for each other, or even enmity.) The news media frequently throws these words around in their reporting. This causes much confusion and strife because the buzzwords tend to have multiple meanings. The news should be concerned with facts, but instead often just generates emotional responses. (Note here that even the words "media" and "news" are buzzwords themselves. I should be more careful when using these two.)

Thus, the mess we are in today is largely linguistic. To fix the problem, people will have to be more thoughtful, logical (and less emotional), and be more careful with the choices of words that they use. The beginnings of a possible solution to the mess begins in the next chapter of this book.

A Possible Solution

The primary thing that we must do is stop the use of buzzwords. How do we begin to do this? The best solution is to ask the person using the buzzword to define it. This does at least three important things:

1) It slows down the conversation (or exchange);

2) It will force the user of the buzzword to stop and think about what they really mean to say. This is key, since the exchange of buzzwords usually shuts down

the thinking process. By asking for a definition, you actually re-start the thinking
process, and an intelligent (and respect-
ful) conversation may ensue; and

3) By slowing down the exchange, you can
actually think of an intelligent and logical
response to the definition as it is given to
you. Thus, we hope that logic, thinking
and listening will supplant emotion and
rancor, and a more civil tone can prevail.

Here is an example of how to achieve a civil conversation about a few current "issues" (or events).
A few weeks ago, I was in a coin store in Ithaca,
New York. The atmosphere in coin (and stamp or
hobby) stores is almost always congenial and
friendly. People there freely swap stories about
coins, stamps, or anything that comes up. There

were two owners present as well as another customer and I. I was talking with one of the owners (a fellow Cornell U. grad), and I said that I was an engineer and an economist.

The other customer interjected, "Engineer and economist? I bet you're a Trump supporter."

Instead of responding immediately, I paused for about 45 seconds. (This gave me a chance to think.) I then responded, "Define 'Trump supporter.'"

He stopped to think for a little while and then responded, "Someone who agrees with everything he does."

I already had had some time to think and I responded, "I don't like everything he does, but here are two things I do like: 1) pushing the Germans to pay a bigger share of NATO expenses; and 2) pulling out of the 'Paris Agreement.'"

Now he stops to think. Then, his response: "I agree with you about NATO, but I'm not sure about the 'Paris Agreement.'"

Wow! We actually have found some common ground on a key political issue and have implicitly "agreed to disagree" on another issue. Note the civility of the tone here. This could have easily turned into angry verbal brawl, but we left the buzzwords in the dust. The conversation continued about coins and stamps, etc. We discovered that we were both Marylanders. I even remember admitting that I was an "old Gerald Ford Republican." I don't think this is a buzzword since it is more precise and did not evoke an emotional response. We parted on good terms and even shook hands.

I even quipped, "Don't mess with the Old Line State!"

Let's think about the above conversation in light of this new conversational strategy.

1) When someone uses a buzzword in the conversation (these words are fairly easy to spot), stop immediately, and slow down the exchange.

2) Ask for a definition. Think.

3) Slow down the exchange, and turn it into a discussion of a few facts or opinions. Think.

4) Be specific. Don't "paint with a broad brush." Think.

5) Find common ground.

6) "Agree to disagree."

7) Above all, be civil.

I believe that if you follow this set of tactics, you will turn many a potentially rancorous exchange into a thoughtful and civil discussion of important events and issues that matter. We can put malice and anger away as we eliminate the use of buzzwords. (Some people will always be angry, so this strategy will not work 100 percent of the time.) Perhaps peace, civility, logic, and thought will return to public and private discourse.

Summary

The cause for much of the angry and foul tone of public and private discourse is rooted in language. The frequent use of a few buzzwords has nearly shut down civil discourse between people of different views and opinions. These buzzwords often evoke strong emotional reactions. Thinking and logic end. Anger rises, and conversations become bitter and soon end. Most people are aware of this but haven't analyzed the pattern carefully.

How do we get out of this messy situation? Here is a strategy:

1) When someone uses a buzzword in the conversation (see Appendix for a partial list), stop immediately and slow down the exchange.

2) Ask for a definition. Stop to think.

3) Slow down the exchange and turn it into a discussion of a few facts or opinions (even one is okay). Think.

4) Be specific. Don't "paint with a broad brush." Think.

5) Find some common ground, if possible.

6) "Agree to disagree."

7) Above all, always be civil. Go slowly, and think about what you mean to say.

What can be the result? Peace, civility, logic, and thought may return to private and public discourse.

Epilogue

How to End the Current Assault
on History and Historical Figures

This might be in the category of "further re-search," but I believe it is related to the subject at hand. I believe the current lack of civility in public and private discourse is related to the current "War on History." Historical figures who may have been regarded as heroes for centuries are now under attack. Some of these attacks even take the form of rioting and mob violence (e.g. Charlottesville).

Whatever your position on the Civil War (and I believe all sides have legitimate viewpoints), we should be able to have a thoughtful and logical discussion about it. (To some people, Robert E. Lee was a great man, and to others, he was a villain.) Maybe both have good reasons. Tearing down statues that have stood for over a century seems to me to be a War on History and also quite ignorant.

The same is true about Christopher Columbus. Why, all of a sudden, does a great historical figure, after centuries of veneration, become an evil villain? This War on History has escalated to attacks on Andrew Jackson. Some people are even attacking George Washington and Thomas Jefferson because they owned slaves. I bet very few people know that even Ulysses S. Grant (the great hero of the Northern Cause in the Civil War and the promoter of Reconstruction) actually owned slaves when he lived in Missouri, less than 20 years before the start of the Civil War. (I hope his memory doesn't come under attack for this.)

People who really know some history are in short supply, and ignorance is advancing. How do we turn this trend around? By promoting thoughtful and logical, civil discourse on these subjects. Throw away the buzzwords.

Appendix

A few commonly used buzzwords:

gun-control	white supremacist
Black Lives Matter	money "laundering"
Blue Lives Matter	drug money
Zionist	Social Justice Warrior (SJW)
Liberal	activist
Conservative	extremist
Socialist	gun "nut"
Communist	NRA
Left-wing	KKK
Right-wing	libtard

Democrat

Republican

dreamer

snowflake

fascist

neo-Nazi

skin head

red neck

Trump supporter

feminist

"the media"

conspiracy theory

libertarian

propaganda

fake news

"the news"

progressive

racist

hate speech

anti-Semite

misogynist

rainbow

trans-gender

tea party

neo-con

alt-right

empowered

ghetto

cracker

entitlements

welfare

About the Author

Thomas Herzfeld is a teacher and economist from Northern New Jersey. He has taught introductory and advanced Economics as well as Statistics at the University of Houston (where he received a Master of Arts degree). He has also taught introductory Micro Economics and the Economics of Money and Banking at Houston Baptist University as well as Macro Economics at San Jacinto Community College (in Houston) and Bergen Community College (Paramus, New Jersey).

He has operated a private tutoring service for more than two decades and has worked on the staff of Passaic County Community College (in Wanaque and Paterson, New Jersey) as a tutor in Mathematics, Statistics, Economics, and Accounting for five years. At the time of writing of this work, he was employed as a Math, Physics, and Economics Teacher at C2 Education (in Livingston, New Jersey).

He is also a graduate of Cornell University with a Bachelor of Science degree in Mechanical and Aerospace Engineering and worked as an engineer in a chemical plant for Shell Oil Co. near Houston, Texas. He also has managerial experience in the retail book business and accounting experience in the imported and wholesale furniture business.

Works by Thomas Herzfeld

Logarithms in 30 Minutes (2018)

Hypothesis Testing Made More Understandable (2018)

How to Have a Civil Conversation in an Increasingly Uncivil and Hostile Environment (2018)

A Leader's Guide to Ensuring Civility in a Hostile Political Environment (2019)

How to Stop the Assault on History (2019)

Basic Trigonometry (without using memorization) (early 2020)

Available on Amazon as Kindle e-books or as paperbacks.